P9-CQA-601

GREAT EXPLORATIONS

La Salle

Down the Mississippi

HAROLD FABER

BENCHMARK **B**OOKS

MARSHALL CAVENDISH
NEW YORK

With special thanks to Stephen Pitti, Assistant Professor of History,
Yale University, for his careful reading of this manuscript.

Benchmark Books
Marshall Cavendish Corporation
99 White Plains Road
Tarrytown, New York 10591-9001

Library of Congress Cataloging-in-Publication Data
Faber, Harold.
La Salle: down the Mississippi by Harold Faber.
p.   cm. – (Great explorations)
Includes bibliographical references and index.
ISBN 0-7614-1239-5
1. La Salle, Robert Cavalier, sieur de, 1643-1687—Juvenile literature. 2. Explorers—North American—Biography—
Juvenile literature. 3. Explorers—France—Biography—Juvenile literature. 4. Canada—Discovery and exploration—
French—Juvenile literature. 5. Canada—History—To 1763 (New France)—Juvenile literature. 6. Mississippi River
Valley—Discovery and exploration—French—Juvenile literature. 7. Mississippi River Valley—History—To 1803—
Juvenile literature. [1. La Salle, Robert Cavalier, sieur de, 1643-1687. 2. Explorers. 3. Canada—Discovery and
exploration—French. 4. Mississippi River—Discovery and exploration.] I. Title. II. Series.
F1030.5 .F33 2001   977'.01'092—dc21   00-051901

Photo Research by Candlepants Incorporated
Cover Photo: Art Resource, Chicago Historical Society
The photographs in this book are used by permission and through the courtesy of; Paul Mellon Collection, © 2001
Board of Trustees National Gallery of Art, Washington: (#1965.16.332) 4, (#1965.16.324) 45, (#1965.16.325) 46,
(#1965.16. 320) 49, (#1965.16.331) 54, (#1965.16.336) 57, (#1965.16.341) 69. Courtesy Center for American
History, U-T Austin: (# 01756) 6, (#09718) 64-65; Corbis: Bettmann , 8, 19, 72; Archivo Iconographic S.A. ,60.
Art Resource NY: Fine Art photographic Library, London, 11; Giraudon, 16, 22, 26; Smithsonian American
Art Museum, Washington DC, 28. National Archives of Canada; (#NAC-C28332), 17 (#NAC-C-6292) 32, 34.
The Granger Collection: 21, 25. Museum of Mobile: 38. Burton Historical Collection of the Detroit Public Library:
41, 42, 66.

Printed in Hong Kong
1   3   5   6   4   2

Contents

On his fourth expedition, La Salle and his men traveled down
the Mississippi River in canoes.

foreword

Historians recognize Robert Cavelier, Sieur de La Salle, better known simply as La Salle, as one of the foremost explorers of America.

In the mid-1600s, he made five expeditions to the interior of what is now the United States, from the Great Lakes to the Gulf of Mexico. Although he was not the discoverer of the Mississippi River, he was the first European to travel down the length of the river. By doing so he opened up a vast area in the middle of the American continent to settlers and trade.

La Salle made his expeditions at the close of a golden period of exploration by Europeans. They did not "discover" America, as some books have said, because America was populated by many tribes and nations of Native Americans.

How could anyone "discover" a land where people already lived?

Historian Samuel Eliot Morison wrote a two-volume work about the early explorers, calling it *The European Discovery of America*. It accurately described the wave of brave sailors from Spain, France, England, Portugal,

La Salle, as imagined by an artist.

and Holland who followed Columbus across the Atlantic Ocean. Their goal was not to explore America, but to find a way around it.

Like Columbus, they were looking for a sea route to the Indies. There, the hot tropical islands close to Asia produced spices like cloves, cinnamon, nutmeg, ginger, and pepper. Because those spices improved the taste of food, they were in great demand in Europe. Merchants who owned ships that could bring the spices back would make a lot of money.

Important Dates in the Early Exploration of America

985   Biarni Heriulfson, first European to discover Labrador.

1000   Leif Ericson, first European to discover Newfoundland.

1492   Columbus, first European to discover America, landing on an island in the Caribbean Sea.

1499   Amerigo Vespucci makes his first voyage to America.

1507   Martin Waldseemüller drafts a map using the word America for the first time.

1513   Ponce de León discovers Florida.

1519   Alonsó de Piñeda discovers the mouth of the Mississippi River.

1524   Giovanni da Verrazzano discovers New York harbor.

1528   Álvar Núñez Cabeza discovers Texas.

1534   Jacques Cartier discovers the St. Lawrence River.

1541   Hernando de Soto crosses the Mississippi River.

1542   Juan Rodríguez Cabrillo discovers California.

1602   Bartholomew Gosnold discovers Cape Cod.

1608   Samuel de Champlain founds Quebec.

1609   Henry Hudson sails up the Hudson River.

1673   Louis Joliet and Jacques Marquette discover the upper Mississippi River.

1678   Louis Hennepin discovers Niagara Falls.

1682   La Salle reaches the mouth of the Mississippi River.

1741   Vitus Jonassen Bering discovers Alaska.

1776   James Cook discovers Hawaii.

1792   Robert Gray discovers the Columbia River.

Jacques Cartier, who discovered the St. Lawrence River in 1535,
with a map of eastern Canada in the background.

They built ships and hired experienced sailors to make the trip. Instead of a quick and easy passage to the Indies, those mariners bumped into a land barrier that they did not know about—America.

Among those early sailors were:

• John Cabot, the first European since Leif Ericson to land in North America, in or near Labrador.

•Amerigo Vespucci, who gave his name to the Americas, in his voyages to Brazil.

•Juan Ponce de León, the first European to set foot in what is now the United States when he landed in Florida.

•Alonsó de Piñeda, who sailed around the coast of the Gulf of Mexico and explored the Mississippi River.

After them came a number of French explorers. Jacques Cartier discovered the St. Lawrence River. He was followed by Samuel Champlain, who founded the city of Quebec on the St. Lawrence River and discovered Lake Champlain in New York State.

Then came Robert Cavelier, Sieur de La Salle, who made several voyages of exploration. We will pay particular attention to La Salle in the following chapters.

ONE

Growing Up in France

When he was born on November 22, 1643, in Rouen, France, he was named René-Robert Cavelier. But he is remembered today as La Salle, after the nickname given to him by his father.

When he came into the world, the French city of Rouen was a busy port. Even though it was a dozen miles from the sea, its location on the Seine River made it a safe harbor for the oceangoing sailing ships of the day.

Because Rouen was such an important port city, it attracted many traders, some from other countries. Because of the busy foreign trade, the local French merchants prospered. They built luxurious town houses for their families, comfortable country estates for relaxation, and a magnificent cathedral in which to worship God.

Among those prosperous families were the Caveliers. La Salle's father, Jean Cavalier, was a merchant in business with his brother,

A street in Rouen, France, in its early days, with the magnificent
Gothic cathedral in the background.

Henri. His mother, Catherine Geest, was a housewife devoted to raising their large family of five boys and a girl.

Their oldest son was named Jean after his father. The next son, Robert, was his father's favorite. As one sign of his high regard for Robert, his father gave him the family property outside the city, La Salle. Thereafter, everybody in the family called the boy La Salle.

Because the Cavaliers were rich, La Salle and his brother Jean grew up in comfortable surroundings. Though the Cavaliers were not a noble family, they lived like lords. They even had associates and friends who were welcomed at the court of Louis XIV, the powerful king of France, in Paris.

Even though their father made his money through trade, neither boy was expected to follow him into the family business. As devout Catholics, the Cavaliers could think of no better career for their sons than that of serving as priests in the church.

Both boys were educated at religious schools. Jean went to a school operated by the order of Sulpician priests. La Salle went to a different school, run by the Society of Jesus, better known simply as the Jesuits, a powerful religious organization.

La Salle's school day was long, from a wake-up call at five o'clock in the morning until nine o'clock at night. He was a good student, with a gift for mathematics and languages. In addition to his religious studies and frequent prayer sessions, he studied astronomy, mapmaking, and six other languages besides his native French: Hebrew, Greek, Latin, Arabic, Spanish, and Italian.

At the age of seventeen, in 1660, he faced a difficult decision: Did he really want to become a priest? His family and teachers all urged him to take his first vows on the road to the priesthood, just as his older brother Jean had done.

Looking back, it seems clear that it was not love of God that determined La Salle's decision. It was the prospect of an adventurous life as a missionary in distant lands like China or India that attracted him. As a Jesuit missionary, he could travel to the far places of the globe. He decided to follow his father's advice and continue his studies for the priesthood.

After he took his vows, the Jesuits sent him to Paris to complete his studies. Unlike his older brother, who submitted to the rigors of the training until he did become a priest, La Salle was a rebel. Although he showed intellectual promise, his superiors worried about him. They did not like his independence of thought and his reluctance to obey church authorities. "He is a restless boy," one disapproving superior wrote.

La Salle stuck it out for six more years. In 1666, he appealed to his superiors for an assignment to China. It was disapproved. He asked to be assigned to Portugal. Disapproved once again. Instead, he was ordered to take advanced studies in theology at a college in Paris.

This was too much for the independent-minded La Salle. He gave up the idea of becoming a priest and resigned from the Jesuits.

The Jesuits recognized that La Salle did not fit in their rigid organization, which operated somewhat like a disciplined army, with priests following orders handed down from above. They accepted his resignation.

What was he to do?

Now twenty-two years old, a grown man, La Salle faced the problem of how to earn a living. When he had entered the Jesuit schools to study for the priesthood, he had signed a vow of poverty, giving up all claims to any share of inheritance from his father. Moreover, his father had just died, so he could not look for help there. Although he was intelligent and well educated, he had neither money nor prospects.

Back in Rouen, La Salle realized that he could not be happy in the trading city, with ships coming from and going to far-off countries. He wanted to go to those places himself! His family—his mother and

ROUEN

The city of Rouen, where La Salle was born, is famous as the place where Joan of Arc was burned at the stake in 1431. Situated on the Seine River, not far from the English Channel, Rouen for centuries has been the port for Paris, the capital of France. When La Salle grew up, it was a busy port with more than a thousand ships a year sailing in and out, as well as a major manufacturing city producing cloth made of linen, hemp, cotton, and silk. It was, and is today, the site of a magnificent Gothic cathedral.

brothers and sisters—decided to step in. They granted him a small annual income, not really enough to live on but enough to start him out in a new life.

Like many other bold and ambitious young men of his time, he decided to look for freedom and adventure across the ocean in New France. His brother Jean had gone there some time before as a priest dedicated to converting the natives to Christianity. La Salle could not do that, but he could take part in exploring and settling New France, the name the French had given to the country we know as Canada.

So in the spring of 1666, he sailed from Rouen to New France to seek his fortune.

T W O

Settling in New France

When La Salle arrived in Montreal in 1666, it was a French outpost in Canada.

At the center of Montreal was a stone fort, built on a high hill called Mont-Royal, from which the city got its name. Between the fort and the St. Lawrence River stood a few wooden houses, a hospital, a small church, and a seminary for the many priests who lived there.

The population was about three hundred, smaller than the bustling city of Rouen from which he had come. Its people were a mixture of priests, Indians, fur traders, merchants, and ambitious young people like La Salle arriving to make a living.

Even though Montreal was thinly populated, its people were sharply divided, with conflicting views on political and social policies. The religious orders—the Jesuits and the Sulpicians—had come as missionaries to convert the Indians to Christianity. But the merchants

What Montreal might have looked like when La Salle arrived.

saw the new continent as a golden opportunity for financial gain. They conducted a busy trade with the Indians for beaver skins, which were in great demand in Europe. La Salle, who was not interested in either religion or money, was motivated solely by the idea of exploration, gaining new lands for France, and glory. Belonging to neither the religious orders nor the fur traders, he became a target of opposition for both groups.

Despite its small size, Montreal was a busy place, a crossroads between France and the interior of the North American continent. It was also the most dangerous place in Canada.

The danger came from the warlike Iroquois tribes of New York to the south. They hated the French because an earlier French explorer, Samuel Champlain, had aided their enemies, the Hurons. As a result, it was hazardous for anyone to venture out of the settlement into the forests around Montreal.

For La Salle, though, New France was mainly an opportunity, not

Some of the first settlers in Montreal were religious men.
Here, Jesuit priests arrive in Quebec in 1625.

BEAVER

The flat-tailed, black-coated beaver sparked much of the exploration of what is now the northern United States and southern Canada. Its furry hide was in great demand in Europe by fashionable people who wanted to wear beaver hats and coats. To supply them, French and English trappers and traders went out into the wilderness of North America either to trap the beaver or trade for it with the Indians. Some of these men were among the first Europeans to contact many Indian tribes, paying them with knives, alcohol, and even rifles in return for the beaver pelts. Without knowing it, they became some of the first explorers of America.

a danger. He was twenty-three years old, ambitious, well educated, proud, and eager. But he had no military training or experience as a leader of men. He did have a connection, though: his brother, Abbé Jean Cavelier, a priest of the Sulpicians, the powerful religious order that ruled Montreal.

The younger Cavelier's ambition, his brother's influence, and the governor's desire to protect Montreal resulted in a grant to La Salle of a large tract of densely forested land—several thousand acres—in the wilderness west of the city. By attracting settlers to the region, La Salle could set up a buffer against Indian attacks.

La Salle's land was just above a place now called Lachine—about seven or eight miles (four to five kilometers) west of Montreal. The St. Lawrence River falls forty-two feet (thirteen meters) in two miles (1.2 kilometers) there, imposing a barrier to any sailing ship trying to go farther up the river. It got its name, then spelled La Chine, as a sort of joke—it was as close as any of the explorers would get to their goal of reaching China.

La Salle's property was vulnerable to attack because it was the closest French settlement to lands still held by Native Americans. But it was still a good starting point for fur traders. They could put their canoes into the St. Lawrence River above the dangerous falls of La Chine, then travel west to where beaver were abundant.

An artist's version of the battle between Huron Indians—led by Samuel Champlain, carrying a rifle in the center of the picture—and Iroquois Indians in 1609 on the shores of Lake Champlain.

Despite his inexperience, La Salle apparently managed the new settlement of La Chine well. He retained about four hundred acres for his own use and rented out the rest in smaller lots to settlers and fur traders. Their first job was difficult. Using only axes, they cleared the land of the pine and larch trees that covered it. Then they built small wooden houses with narrow windows as protection against Indian arrows.

Even though the land was not suitable for growing crops, La Salle and the other settlers found that they could feed themselves easily. For experienced hunters, deer and moose were abundant in the forests around them and made good eating.

An adventurous man, La Salle left La Chine often to explore the forest. He quickly found that his European clothes and shoes were not suitable for tramping in the woods. He substituted soft Indian moccasins for the hard leather shoes that he used in France and wore leather leggings to protect his legs from the sharp undergrowth between the trees. He wrote to a friend back in France:

> One doesn't wear a sword in this country as it is an encumbrance when walking in the woods, and useless against the hatchets usually carried there—the savages have the strength to throw their hatchets thirty paces with such skill that they ordinarily bury the steel within the skull of anyone they designate.

For La Salle, the first two years at La Chine were almost like going to school to learn how to live in the wilderness. In the summertime, he covered his body with bear grease to protect himself against the many mosquitoes and flies. When he was hungry, he learned to follow woodpeckers to trees and strip the bark where they had been pecking. Beneath the bark were colonies of carpenter ants that he scooped out and ate. In the winter, which was much colder than anything he had known in France, La Salle used homemade snowshoes in the woods.

In winter, French Canadians often traveled on
homemade showshoes, like those shown here.

He wore a long wool scarf to cover his mouth, a beaver skin hat pulled down over his ears, and mittens to protect his hands. With snow on the ground, it was easy to follow the tracks of animals and set traps to catch them for food.

His immediate problem was the protection of the new settlement of La Chine. He built a small fort as a barrier to hostile Indians, but he also studied the languages of friendly Indians who came to trade their furs.

La Salle's settlement was subject to attack by hostile Indians, such as the Iroquois pictured here.

WHERE DID THE NAME CANADA COME FROM?

In 1535, Jacques Cartier, the first French explorer of the St. Lawrence River, stopped his ships at an Indian village called Stadaconé (the site of what was to become the present city of Quebec). When he asked the natives what they called it, they replied, "Cannata."

Cartier used a version of that word, Canada, to mean the entire region. It soon came to be the name of the entire country.

From them, he heard about a great river to the west called the Ohio that they said flowed into the sea. La Salle thought this meant that it flowed into the Gulf of California, thus providing a gateway to the Pacific Ocean and China beyond.

Like all explorers of his day, La Salle dreamed of being the one to discover a North American water route to the Indies. He decided that he would do it. Three years after his arrival in New France, La Salle was ready to begin his life as an explorer.

THREE

The First Expedition

Before La Salle could organize an expedition to find a water route to China, he had to get permission from the governor of New France. La Salle traveled to Quebec, where he convinced the governor that the proposed exploration would expand the frontiers of New France.

His plan was approved, but with two conditions: he had to pay for the trip himself and to combine his expedition with another preparing to leave Montreal at about the same time. This second expedition was strictly religious, led by two priests. Unhappy at the fact that he was not to have complete command of the combined expedition, La Salle was nevertheless forced to accept the conditions.

Quebec, the largest city of New France, as seen from the St. Lawrence River.

He persuaded the Sulpician order to buy back the property it had given him because he had cleared and improved the land for settlement. With the money, he bought four canoes and supplies for the trip. He also hired fourteen men for a fifteen-month period. The two priests contributed three canoes, which they loaded up with medical supplies to use in their dealings with the Indians.

On July 6, 1669, twenty-four men in seven large canoes—accompanied by Seneca Indian guides in two small canoes—set out from La Chine. Their route was up the narrow St. Lawrence River, where boulders and fallen trees frequently blocked their passage. When that

Jacques Cartier was the first to sail down the St. Lawrence River. Here, his "discovery" of the river in 1535 is depicted.

happened, they had to portage—take the canoes out of the water and carry them around the obstacles.

Traveling was not easy. Surrounded by clouds of insects, branches slashing at their faces, the men paddled or portaged all day long. At night they went ashore to make camp. One of the priests described what happened then:

> *If the weather is fair you make a fire and lie down to sleep without further trouble; but, if it rains, you must peel bark from the trees and make a shed by laying it on a frame of sticks. As for your food, it is enough to make you burn all cookery books that ever were written; for in the woods of Canada one finds means to live well without bread, wine, salt, pepper or spices. The ordinary food is Indian corn, or Turkey wheat as it is called in France, which is crushed between two stones and boiled, seasoning it with meat or fish, when you can get them.*

On August 2, twenty-seven days after they left La Chine, the expedition reached the mouth of the St. Lawrence River at the eastern end of Lake Ontario. Continuing on, they hugged the south shore of the lake until they reached Irondequoit Bay, near the present-day city of Rochester. There they met a band of friendly Seneca Indians.

Although they were received politely, La Salle and his companions were shocked at some of the Indian customs. They watched with horror, for example, as a prisoner was tied to a stake and tortured by fire for six hours, while the Senecas danced and yelled with delight. Then the captive's body was cut up, boiled, and eaten.

Fearful for their own safety and unable to find guides to lead them to the Ohio River, La Salle and the others left. They paddled their canoes to the end of Lake Ontario, arriving near the present-day town of Hamilton, Canada, in late September.

There La Salle, who was a reserved man with few intimates, made

A warrior of the Seneca tribe of Indians, who were friendly to La Salle.

a friend who stayed with him for the rest of his life. The Indians he met gave him a captive Shawnee Indian named Nika. La Salle and Nika got along beautifully. They walked together, talking and learning each other's languages. Nika told him the Ohio River was not far away and that it could be reached in six weeks.

For La Salle, this was good news. Even better news came from a fur trader they met who was traveling from the west back to Montreal. After showing maps he had made of lakes to the west, the trader told

Previous French Explorers

Before La Salle made his expeditions, two other French explorers had opened the way to the interior of North America, Jacques Cartier (1491–1557) and Samuel Champlain (1567–1635).

Cartier, a master mariner, made his first trip across the Atlantic Ocean in 1534, seeking a route to the Indies. He did not find it, but he did discover the Gulf of St. Lawrence and many of the islands in it. On his second voyage, in 1535, Cartier sailed into what the natives called the Great River of Hochelaga. We now know it as the St. Lawrence River. Cartier made one more voyage, in 1541. On that trip, his ships were stopped from further exploration by the La Chine Falls, west of Montreal. French exploration of the region halted while France was divided by religious wars.

More than fifty years later, Samuel Champlain, another French master mariner, sailed into the St. Lawrence River. After several trips back and forth to France, he convinced the king to set up a colony in Canada. In 1608, he built a settlement at what became the city of Quebec. As the founder of the first permanent French settlement in North America, Champlain is called the father of "New France," or Canada.

the priests that the Potawatomi Indians and other tribes of the region needed spiritual assistance.

Because of that, the La Salle expedition broke in two. The priests headed west on their religious mission to convert more Indians to Christianity.

La Salle, happy at being in command for the first time, did not give up his dream of discovering the river that led to the sea. Instead of going back to Montreal, he and his men spent the winter in huts they built south of Lake Ontario.

In the spring of 1670, they carried their canoes overland for a short distance until they found a stream running south. When they reached their goal, the Ohio River, they found it to be filled with rocks, tree trunks, and debris, with many eddies and waterfalls.

Their progress down the river was difficult and slow. It was frequently necessary to carry their canoes through water up to their waists because the banks of the river, as well as the river itself, were an impossible tangle of roots, trees, and branches. They were attacked by horseflies and mosquitoes, and they had to be careful to avoid rattlesnakes on the banks.

Obsessed by his dream of reaching the ocean, La Salle pushed on until he was stopped by the falls at the present site of Louisville, Kentucky. Although La Salle's drive brought him closer to his objective, it also led to a silent mutiny.

La Salle had ignored the grumbling of his men and their resentment of his stern orders. Finally they would take no more of him. One night, all the men silently disappeared. They left La Salle and his faithful companion Nika alone in the wilderness.

This episode illustrated two traits of La Salle's character, one negative, the other positive.

On this as on all of his expeditions, he did not show the kind of leadership that would win the support of the men under him. He did not make the effort to become friendly with the rough, independent-minded Frenchmen he had to work with. Curiously, he acted more warmly toward the Indians he met, and he got along very well with them.

On the positive side, La Salle showed his tough spirit after he was deserted near Louisville. Physically fit from his training at La Chine, he found the inner strength to carry on through the wilderness. He and Nika hunted for game, dug roots to eat, set snares to catch game, and they survived. Together, La Salle and Nika returned to Montreal in the winter of 1670.

Back in Montreal, La Salle found that a new governor had arrived from France, Louis de Buade, Count de Frontenac. For the next several years, he played an important role in La Salle's life.

Frontenac shared La Salle's vision of finding the great river to the west that led to the Pacific Ocean. If the French discovered it, they could extend their control of North America at the expense of their rivals, the English and the Spanish. French possession of the middle of America would restrict the English to settlements along the Atlantic coastline and keep the Spanish bottled up in Mexico and the southwest.

Frontenac sent out another expedition to explore the west. Its leaders were a priest, Jacques Marquette, often called Père (Father) Marquette, and a young fur trapper, Louis Joliet.

On May 17, 1673, they set out in canoes to explore the many waterways west of Montreal to Lake Michigan. When they reached Green Bay, they paddled up the Fox River, crossed Lake Winnebago, then carried their canoes overland to the Wisconsin River. Exactly one month after they started, on June 17, they entered a broad river near the present-day city of Prairie du Chien. Marquette and Joliet had discovered the northern Mississippi River.

Père Marquette and Louis Joliet discovering the northern
Mississippi River in 1673.

They went down the river far enough to convince themselves that it flowed south into the Gulf of Mexico, not west into the Pacific Ocean. Joliet returned to Quebec to report the good news to Frontenac while Marquette remained behind on his mission to convert the Indians to Christianity. The next step in the French exploration of the Mississippi fell to La Salle.

At that time La Salle was not yet thirty years old. We do not know what he looked like or the color of his hair or eyes because no contemporary portrait of him has been found. From his actions, we do know that he was determined, strong, and an able woodsman, capable of surviving adverse conditions in the wilderness. A quiet man, he had few friends and many enemies. Jealous of his success, his enemies charged that he was a schemer, that he traded where he had no right to trade, that his discoveries were only a pretense for making money, and that he was harsh toward his men. La Salle denied those charges, but some of them were true.

He obviously was interested in making money to pay back the friends and relatives who had invested in his expeditions, but he never showed any sign of trying to accumulate wealth for himself. Was he harsh toward his men? Sometimes. As commander, he felt he had to maintain order among tough men who were frequently drunk and disorderly. He wrote to a friend in France: "It will not be found that I have in any case treated any man harshly, except for blasphemies and other such crimes, openly committed. These I cannot tolerate."

La Salle knew he was not popular. "If I am wanting in expansiveness and show of feeling toward those with whom I associate, it is only through a timidity which is natural to me," he wrote in another letter. He was surrounded by enemies, and therefore, he said, "It is not surprising that I open my mind to nobody, and distrust everybody."

Despite all that, he and Frontenac became close associates with a shared ambition: to open the heartland of North America to French trade and settlement. Frontenac's first step was to build a fort on Lake Ontario near where the St. Lawrence River started. A fort and trading post there would make it easier for the Indians of the Great Lakes region to trade their furs to Frenchmen rather than to the English in New York. The site, recommended by La Salle, is now the city of Kingston.

For La Salle, becoming the commander of the new Fort Frontenac would present a great opportunity. In 1674, he sailed back to France

An early map of Fort Frontenac. The fort was built by La Salle on the northern shore of Lake Ontario.

Crossing the Atlantic

Today it is easy to cross the Atlantic Ocean by airplane in a few hours. But in La Salle's day, the only means of ocean transportation was on small, slow sailing ships.

If the weather was good and the winds favorable, you could sail from France to Newfoundland in twenty days. If the weather was bad, as it frequently was in the North Atlantic, the trip could take fifty to sixty or more days. Because the winter weather was bad so often, many ships were lost at sea, overturned in storms or sunk after hitting icebergs.

La Salle was lucky at sea. Despite his many trips back and forth to France, he never, as far as we know, ran into any serious trouble.

to obtain that post. He carried a letter from Count Frontenac to Jean-Baptiste Colbert, the king's chief minister, recommending him as

a man of intelligence and ability, more capable of anybody else I know here to accomplish every kind of enterprise and discovery which may be entrusted to him, as he has the most perfect knowledge of the state of this country, as you will see.

At the French court, La Salle made two requests: first, in consideration of his services as an explorer, to be raised to the rank of nobility, and second, to be granted command of Fort Frontenac. Both requests were granted, with several conditions: He had to pay for everything himself, rebuild the fort in stone, open the land around it to settlers, and build a church. Encouraged by the king's support, friends and relatives lent him money for the new enterprise.

La Salle's new role found a mixed reception in Montreal. Frontenac was delighted, but some of his associates were not. The other fur traders were angry because they saw La Salle becoming a major competitor, with his key position at Fort Frontenac. And the Jesuits became openly hostile, because they felt that their dominant position in the Great Lakes was threatened by La Salle's new appointment.

In spite of that opposition, La Salle spent the next two years fulfilling his obligation to make Fort Frontenac a strong outpost of New France. Under his direction, a stone fort was built. Land was cleared and a group of settlers came to farm. A flour mill and a bakery were built. Indians and fur traders flocked in from the west, and the new fort prospered.

"If he had preferred gain to glory, he had only to stay at his fort, where he was making more than twenty-five thousand livres a year," one of his associates wrote. Although it is impossible today to put an exact value on that amount of money, it was a fortune, enough to make La Salle a rich man if he chose to stay there.

But La Salle still dreamed. By this time, he had become convinced that the great river to the west did not lead to the Pacific Ocean, but rather to the Gulf of Mexico. He saw that river as the backbone of a new French empire in America. To gain permission to explore it and set up forts that would guarantee French possession, he again went to France to get permission from the king.

f O U R

The Second Expedition

In 1677, La Salle sailed back to France. He made a very good impression at the French court as he presented his proposal for further exploration. One of the observers there described him as a man of "great intelligence and good sense." Soon, the king gave his answer:

> *Louis, by the grace of God King of France and Navarre, to our dear and well-beloved Robert Cavelier, Sieur de La Salle, greeting. We have received with favor the very humble petition made us in your name, to permit you to labor at the discovery of the western parts of New France....*

Specifically, La Salle received the right to build forts in the areas he discovered. He also was granted a monopoly in the trade of buffalo skins, which were in great demand in Europe. But the king gave him no money. Since he had to pay for everything himself, he again turned

Henri de Tonty, La Salle's trusted deputy and friend.

to family. "His brothers and relations spared him nothing to enable him to respond worthily to the royal goodness," one observer said.

In France, La Salle made a new friend, Henri de Tonty (sometimes spelled Tonti), who became a trusted ally and his second in command. Tonty had an unusual disability, which made him feared by the Indians he met in America. An experienced Italian army officer, he had lost a hand in battle as the result of a grenade explosion. To mask his loss, he wore an artificial hand made of iron, covered with a glove. Using his iron hand occasionally as a weapon to knock out an opponent, Tonty made a deep impression on the Indians. They looked up to him as a powerful "medicine" man.

La Salle quickly organized his expedition. He bought supplies of iron, sails, and ropes and hired the carpenters and blacksmiths needed to build a ship for his new exploration. With Tonty and a crew of experienced shipbuilders, he arrived back in New France in September 1678.

It would have been easy to build a ship on Lake Ontario, but there was an impassable barrier to sailing it farther west: Niagara Falls. Halfway between Lakes Ontario and Erie on the Niagara River, it was an awesome spectacle to the French who discovered it. But for La Salle Niagara Falls was an obstacle to be overcome.

As an experienced commander, La Salle sent out two advance crews. One went to build a fort at the foot of the Niagara River, where it flows into Lake Ontario. The other scouted out a suitable site for boat building on Lake Erie, on the far side of Niagara Falls. Transporting the supplies from Fort Niagara by land around Niagara Falls was hard work in the winter of 1678–1679.

Despite the cold, snow, and ice, La Salle's shipbuilders completed their work under the direction of his trusted lieutenant, Tonty. La Salle was absent because he had to rush back to Montreal to satisfy his creditors, who had seized all his property to pay his debts. But he was able to convince them that he had enough assets at Fort Frontenac to

Niagara Falls

As part of La Salle's second expedition, Father Louis Hennepin became the first European to gaze upon Niagara Falls—on December 6, 1678—and describe it.

He later wrote: "We entered the beautiful river Niagara, which no bark had ever yet entered. . . . There is an incredible Cataract or Waterfall, which has no equal. The Niagara River near this place is only an eighth of a mile wide, but it is very deep in places and so rapid above the great fall, that it hurries all animals which try to cross it without a single one being able to withstand its current."

At that first sight, Hennepin exaggerated the height of the falls, estimating it at five hundred feet (152 meters). In reality, it is only 190 feet (58 meters).

pay them and that he would have even more when his expedition returned.

On August 7, 1679, the new ship was ready to sail. She was fifty feet (fifteen meters) long and sixteen feet (five meters) wide, with two masts for sails, armed with five cannons. She was named the *Griffin* (sometimes spelled *Griffon*), after the fabulous creature with the wings of an eagle and the body of a lion that was depicted on the coat of arms of the Count de Frontenac.

Niagara Falls, in a woodcut published in 1698.

With sails unfurled, the *Griffin* sailed west on Lake Erie, the first sailing ship ever seen on the Great Lakes. For the Indians on the shore, the *Griffin* was a fantastic sight. The huge ship with its billowing white sails was a spectacle beyond their imagining.

The *Griffin* found favorable winds and made good time. She took three days to reach the eastern end of Lake Erie, then turned north through the Strait of Detroit and Lake St. Clair into Lake Huron.

A week later, the ship reached Michilimackinac, a Jesuit outpost on the island between Lakes Huron and Michigan. To impress the Indians there, La Salle fired the *Griffin's* cannon. Then he marched ashore, dressed in a colorful mantle of scarlet bordered with gold.

The Second Expedition

After a short stay, La Salle set sail again in September for his next destination, Green Bay on the western shore of Lake Michigan. Good news awaited him. An advance group of his men had collected a big stockpile of furs, ready to be shipped back to Montreal.

La Salle saw an opportunity to sell the furs for a large amount of money to pay off his creditors—and made a major mistake. He decided to send the *Griffin*, loaded with furs, back east to Niagara while he continued his exploration to the south.

On September 18, the *Griffin* set sail, with orders to return to Lake

Construction of the Griffin, La Salle's ship built to sail upon the Great Lakes, with La Salle in the center and a carving of a griffin on the ship's stern.

The Second Expedition

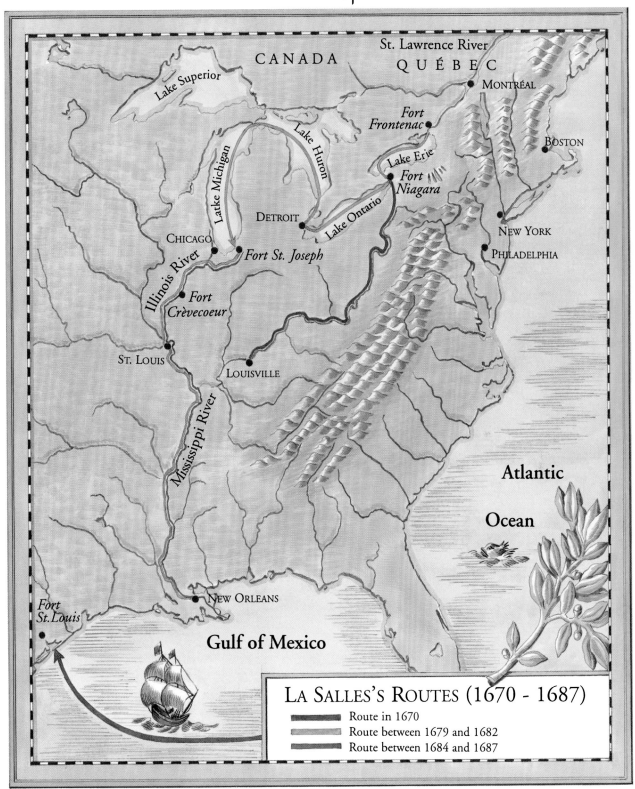

Michigan as soon as she had discharged her cargo of furs. Unfortunately for La Salle, the *Griffin* disappeared. Presumably she sank in a storm on Lake Michigan.

Some skeptics say that is too easy an explanation of her disappearance. They speculate that her crew saw an opportunity to make a fortune for themselves by stealing the furs to sell to the English and Dutch. To hide their crime, this story goes, they sank the ship in the deep waters of the lake.

No one knows what really happened. To this day, no trace of the *Griffin*, her crew, or her cargo has ever been found.

Later in September 1679, La Salle left Green Bay to continue his exploration. His expedition consisted of fourteen men in four canoes loaded with tools, hatchets, knives, and arms to be used as trading goods with the Indians.

It was not easy going, paddling through the sudden storms that came up on Lake Michigan. The usually calm lake was hit by sudden squalls that almost overturned their canoes. La Salle and his men were driven ashore several times by high waves and gusty winds. Wet, hungry, and tired, they huddled around fires at night, living on pumpkins and Indian corn.

They pushed on to the southern end of Lake Michigan until they reached the mouth of the St. Joseph River, east of present-day Chicago. There they built a crude fort of logs, Fort St. Joseph. Tonty arrived on November 20 with more men and supplies. La Salle's expedition now consisted of thirty-three men in eight canoes.

On December 3, they left, canoeing up the St. Joseph River, looking for a water route to the Mississippi. On the advice of an Indian guide, they pulled their canoes out of the water and carried them five miles (three kilometers) over land to another river, the Kanakee, near the present site of South Bend, Indiana.

From the Kanakee, La Salle passed into the Illinois River. On January

La Salle and his crew arriving at an Indian village
on the Illinois River in 1680.

5, 1680, they reached a widening of the river, Peoria Lake. In front of them was a large village, consisting of about eighty wigwams. The Indians were surprised at the sight of eight canoes bearing down on them. Some whooped and hollered, some seized their arrows and war clubs, fearing an attack.

La Salle leaped ashore, followed by his men, prepared for battle.

But fighting was avoided when two chiefs came forward bearing pipes of peace. La Salle, in turn, displayed his pipe. The Indians placed food in front of them. In turn, the Frenchmen gave the Indians tobacco and hatchets.

After a feast, La Salle and his men were lodged in nearby huts. When La Salle arose the next morning, he found that six of his men had deserted. Discontented with the hardships of the trip, they obviously preferred traveling through the wintry weather back to New France over facing the unknown dangers ahead.

And that was not all. Someone tried to kill La Salle by putting poison in one of the pots in which his food was cooked. Tonty later

Sailing on the Illinois River in 1680, La Salle came to a large Indian village. Although he feared an attack, the Indians proved their friendliness by preparing a feast for La Salle and his crew.

reported that he was saved only by using a medicine that a friend had given him before he left France.

Historian Francis Parkman explained that La Salle, so skillful in his dealing with Indians, was rarely so with his own countrymen. The desertions from which he was continually to suffer were due both to his own haughty conduct and to the difficulty of traveling in the wilderness. Parkman wrote:

> In those early French enterprises in the West, it was to the last degree difficult to hold men to their duty. Once fairly in the wilderness, completely freed from the restraints of authority in which they had passed their lives, a spirit of lawlessness broke out among them.

With winter upon him, La Salle knew he could go no farther. On a low hill beyond the Indian camp, he erected a square fort. Its wooden walls were twenty-five feet (eight meters) high and a foot (thirty centimeters) thick, sunk three feet (one meter) into the ground. Inside were wooden huts for the men, separate huts for La Salle, Tonty, and the priests, a forge, and a magazine for arms and ammunition.

La Salle named it Fort Crèvecoeur (French for "brokenhearted"). It was the first European settlement in what is now the state of Illinois.

FIVE

The Third Expedition

During the winter, La Salle divided his men into three groups. The first consisted of Michel Accau, Father Louis Hennepin, and a few others. Their mission was to travel down the Illinois River in canoes to find the Mississippi River. The second was led by Tonty, who remained behind at Fort Crèvecoeur. His job was to finish a large new boat that would later take La Salle down the Illinois River. La Salle himself led the third group, which included Nika and four other Frenchmen he could trust. They set out in two canoes to return to Fort Frontenac for the anchors, cables, rigging, and sails needed for the new boat.

It was a miserable trip in the winter snow, ice, and freezing rain. When they could, La Salle and his party paddled their canoes in rivers nearly covered by broken ice. When the rivers were frozen over, they carried the canoes over land through deep snow. They trudged through

In the winter of 1680, La Salle returned to Fort Frontenac after
an epic sixty-five-day trek through snow and ice.

icy rain that froze their clothes to their bodies. All the while, they dodged hostile Indian war parties.

Parkman described La Salle's journey:

During sixty-five days, he had toiled almost incessantly, traveling, by the course he took, about a thousand miles through a country beset with every form of peril and obstruction.

It was "the most arduous journey," says the chronicler, "ever made by a Frenchman in America."

When La Salle reached Montreal on May 6, 1680, he was met with only bad news. His creditors had seized his property, a ship bringing supplies from France had sunk in the Gulf of St. Lawrence, and several of his canoes had been lost in the rapids of the St. Lawrence River. In addition, two messengers arrived with a most distressing letter from Tonty: Nearly all the men left behind at Fort Crèvecoeur had deserted after burning the fort. Tonty and his loyal men had fled into the wilderness.

At that point, a weaker man might have abandoned any plans for further exploration. But La Salle, now thirty-seven years old, did not despair. He convinced his creditors and friends to finance a new expedition. He was determined to find his faithful friend Tonty and together travel down the Mississippi River.

On August 22, 1680, La Salle departed on his third expedition to the west. His new company consisted of twenty-five men, including some experienced shipbuilders and carpenters to complete the boat Tonty was building at Fort Crèvecoeur. They traveled down the route he knew so well to the Illinois River.

They found devastation. Villages of the friendly Illinois Indians had been burned to the ground. Fields were strewn with broken bones and corpses. Skeletons had been pulled from their graves and left to rot on the ground.

La Salle knew that the Iroquois nation had been on the warpath. As

WHO WAS THE FIRST EUROPEAN TO SAIL THE MISSISSIPPI RIVER?

A Spanish mariner, Alonso Alvarez de Piñeda led a fleet of three ships around the coast of the Gulf of Mexico in 1518. In 1519, he came to a large river—the Mississippi—and went about twenty miles (twelve kilometers) up it. But then he turned around and sailed on to Mexico.

From 1539 to 1541, Hernando de Soto led a Spanish army by land through what is now the southwestern United States, looking for gold. He never found any, but on May 21, 1541, he reached a wide river that he called Rio del Espiritu Santo (River of the Holy Ghost). It was the Mississippi. For de Soto and his men, it was not a major discovery, only an obstacle that had to be crossed.

More than a hundred years later, on June 17, 1673, two Frenchmen came to the upper Mississippi River. Together, Jacques Marquette and Louis Joliet had crossed the Great Lakes in birch bark canoes and followed a series of small rivers to the Mississippi.

The next French explorer, La Salle, followed them in 1681–1682.

rulers of the area south of the St. Lawrence River, they enforced their rule ruthlessly. "They are politically minded, wily, treacherous, vindictive and cruel to their enemies, whom they burn on a slow fire with incredible torment," he wrote to a friend in Paris.

As he examined the bodies of the victims, La Salle could find no sign of Tonty or the other Frenchmen. He continued on to Fort Crèvecoeur, which had been razed, as he expected. Surprisingly, though, the boat under construction had not been destroyed.

La Salle continued on down the Illinois River. After a short time, in December 1680, he reached its mouth, where the Illinois flowed into the broad Mississippi, the object of his dreams. But he worried about Tonty. His men suggested that they follow the Mississippi to the sea. La Salle refused. His first duty was to his trusted ally. He had to find out what had happened to Tonty and his loyal followers. So the day after Christmas, he turned back.

S I X

The fourth Expedition

The journey back to Fort St. Joseph was made in the coldest winter La Salle had ever seen. He wrote:

> *I have never suffered so much from the cold, or had more trouble in getting forward; for the snow was so light, resting suspended as it were among the tall grass, that we could not use snowshoes. Sometimes it was waist deep; and as I walked before my men, as usual, to encourage them by breaking the path, I had much ado, although I am rather tall, to lift my legs above the drifts.*

Back in Fort St. Joseph, La Salle displayed another of his strengths by organizing many friendly tribes into an alliance to protect themselves—and the French—against the powerful Iroquois nation. Needing no interpreter because he spoke the Indian languages, he persuaded

La Salle's trip back to Fort St. Joseph was brutally cold. Here,
La Salle and his party are pictured crossing the ice on a frozen lake.

them to make peace among themselves and to support the French.

With the coming of spring, La Salle traveled north by canoe on Lake
Michigan to Michilimackinac, where he held a joyous reunion with
Tonty.

After the destruction of Fort Crèvecoeur, Tonty had had a most
difficult time surviving. He had reached a friendly Illinois village, but
had soon found himself in the middle of a battle between the Illinois
and Iroquois. He later wrote:

The Fourth Expedition

I was never in such perplexity, for at that moment there was an Iroquois behind me, lifting my hair as if he were going to scalp me. I thought it was all over for me, and that my best hope was that they would knock me in the head instead of burning me, as I believed they would do.

Luckily for him, the Iroquois decided to release Tonty rather than cause more friction by killing a Frenchman.

Together, La Salle and Tonty set out to return to Fort Frontenac and Montreal to gather supplies for another Mississippi expedition. With the help of Count de Frontenac, La Salle once more persuaded his creditors to wait for their payments. He even raised more money to finance the new expedition.

In September 1681, La Salle left on his fourth expedition. His party consisted of twenty-three Frenchmen, including Tonty, and thirty-one Indians, including Nika. La Salle had given up his idea of using a large boat, and they traveled by canoe.

By now their route was familiar to them. They reached the Illinois River on December 28 and the Mississippi on February 6, 1682.

After all their previous troubles, the trip down the Mississippi was peaceful. As the weather became milder, La Salle's crew was well fed and cheerful. There was an abundance of game on the shore, including herds of buffalo. Farther south, they saw their first alligators and killed them for food, too. They met friendly Indians and once again, La Salle displayed his ability to make friends of the natives. One of his party later wrote:

The Sieur de La Salle, whose very air, engaging manners, tact and address attract love and respect alike, produced such an effect on the hearts of these people that they did not know how to treat us well enough.

On April 6, La Salle came to three branches in the Mississippi, south of where New Orleans is today. He divided his party into three groups. He traveled down the west fork, Tonty took the middle, and another crew member went down the east.

La Salle soon came to salt water and the open sea. He had reached the Gulf of Mexico.

Three days later, the entire crew gathered at the site where the Mississippi broke into the three branches. Following the custom of the times, they carved these words into a tree:

Louis Le Grande, Roy de France et de Navarre, Règne:
Le Neuvième Avril, 1682.
(Louis the Great, King of France and Navarre, Reigns Here:
April 9, 1682).

In a loud voice, La Salle proclaimed:

In the name of the most high, mighty, invincible, and victorious Prince, Louis the Great, by the grace of God King of France and of Navarre, Fourteenth of that name, I, on this ninth day of April, 1682, in virtue of the commission of His Majesty, which I hold in my hand, and which may be seen by all whom it may concern, have taken and now do take in the name of his Majesty and all of his successors to the crown, possession of this country of Louisiana, the seas, harbors, ports, bays, adjacent straits, and all of the nations, peoples, provinces, cities, towns, villages, mines, minerals, fisheries, streams and rivers within the extent of the said Louisiana.

With those words, La Salle did two things: First, he claimed for France the vast basin of the Mississippi River, from the woody ridges of the Allegheny Mountains in the east to the snowy peaks of the Rocky Mountains in the west, from Canada in the north to the Gulf of Mexico

After arriving at the mouth of the Mississippi River on April 9, 1682, La Salle claimed the entire area for France and named it Louisiana.

in the south. Second, he named that vast area Louisiana in honor of King Louis XIV of France. It would not become part of the United States until 1803 with the Louisiana Purchase.

S E V E N

Hostility and Honor

On April 10, 1862, the day after the ceremony, La Salle began the return trip up the Mississippi River. He sent Tonty ahead to dispatch news of their discovery to Quebec, but he himself was delayed by sickness. He wrote to a friend later:

> Though my discovery is made, and I have descended the Mississippi to the Gulf of Mexico, I cannot send you this year either an account of my journey or a map. On the way back, I was attacked by a deadly disease which kept me in danger of my life for forty days, and left me so weak that I could think of nothing for four months after.

After recovering from his illness, probably malaria, he met Tonty on the banks of the Illinois River, not far from the site of Fort Crève-coeur. They decided to build a new fort at Starved Rock, an outcropping 115 feet (about 18 meters) high above the river, as a base for the

King Louis XIV of France.

expansion of commerce down the Mississippi. They called it Fort St. Louis.

It was here that La Salle learned that instead of being regarded as a hero back in Quebec, he was on the verge of ruin. His mentor, Count de Frontenac, had been called back to France. His replacement envied La Salle, who had a monopoly on the fur trade near the forts that he had built.

The new governor, Le Febvre de la Barre, was old, weak, and incompetent. He confiscated all of La Salle's property at Fort Frontenac and relieved him of command of both that fort and the new Fort St. Louis.

La Salle saw that the only way he could continue his work was to go to Paris and speak to the king himself. In November 1682, he sailed back to France.

In contrast to his hostile reception in Quebec, La Salle was treated like a hero in France. Everyone wanted to hear about his adventures on the Mississippi River. La Salle had returned at just the right time. France was on the verge of war with Spain. King Louis and his ministers were delighted to hear La Salle's proposals to build a fort at the mouth of the Mississippi, to settle the land along the river, and to form an alliance with the Indians to attack the Spanish. To do all that, La Salle asked the king to supply him with a warship, a few cannons for the fort, and two hundred men to be armed and maintained at the king's expense.

King Louis responded most generously, giving La Salle even more than he asked for. First, he ordered the governor in New France to return Fort Frontenac and Fort St. Louis to La Salle. Second, he named La Salle commander of all the territory between the Illinois River and the Spanish possessions in New Mexico. Third, instead of the single ship that La Salle requested, he gave him four ships: a thirty-six gun warship, the *Joly*; a smaller ship with six guns, the *Belle*; a large supply ship, the *Amiable*; and a smaller supply ship, the *St. François*. Fourth, to man the new expedition, the king ordered a hundred soldiers to accompany

A Bachelor

La Salle never married, but when he was in his late thirties he almost did. One of the landowners at Fort Frontenac was Madeleine de Roybon d'Allonne, a woman a few years younger than he. She had presumably come to New France to find a husband.

La Salle was interested, but he was more interested in his explorations. He wrote to a friend in France that he could not think of marriage until he had completed his mission on the Mississippi River. Despite his reluctance, Mademoiselle d'Allonne had so much faith in La Salle that she even helped finance his expeditions.

After La Salle's death, she lived a dramatic life. She was captured by Iroquois Indians in 1687 and remained a captive for several years. When she was finally released, she returned to Montreal and then to Paris to sue to regain her farm at Fort Frontenac. By the time she won her suit, she was too weak to return to the farm. She died in Montreal in 1718 at the age of seventy-two.

La Salle, as well as mechanics, laborers, a number of young orphaned girls (who it was thought would find husbands in the new land), and several priests. In addition to the ships'crews, the expedition consisted of about three hundred men, women, and children.

Because the ships were part of the royal navy, the king's ministers divided the leadership of the expedition. It was to sail directly across the Atlantic Ocean to the Gulf of Mexico, a more practical route than via the St. Lawrence River, the Great Lakes, and then down the length of the Mississippi River. Once the ships landed at the Gulf of Mexico, La Salle was to be in sole command. But at sea, Captain Taneguy de Beaujeu, a veteran naval officer, commanded the ships. It was a prudent decision, because La Salle had no experience as a mariner. But, like all divided commands, it led to friction.

EIGHT

The fifth Expedition

On July 24, 1684, La Salle sailed from France on his fifth and last expedition — and into trouble.

La Salle and Captain Beaujeu quarreled constantly about almost everything—how to load the ships, where to stop for supplies, how to avoid the Spanish, and where to land. On the long voyage, many of the men took sick, and some even died. La Salle himself came down with a high fever, possibly a recurrence of his malaria.

To add to their troubles, the expedition entered waters controlled by Spain, France's enemy. Although they landed safely in Santo Domingo for supplies, they lost one of their ships, the small *St. François*, to Spanish pirates.

With only three ships left, they sailed around Cuba and into the Gulf of Mexico. Their goal was the mouth of the Mississippi River, but because of inexperience and the crude navigational tools of their day,

they missed it. They continued until December 28, when a sailor on the masthead of the *Amiable* sighted land ahead.

La Salle looked out at the flat, barren, sandy landscape, with no recognizable features. He decided to go on. After weeks of fruitless

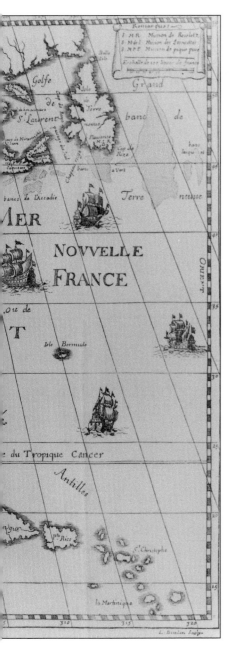

A 1692 map of New France, showing some obvious errors. Here the Mississippi River is located far west of its actual mouth at the Gulf of Mexico.

sailing, La Salle entered Matagorda Bay, on the far western shores of the Gulf of Mexico. He landed there, believing he was close to the Mississippi River. He was wrong—he was four hundred miles (250 kilometers) west of his goal, almost at the border of present-day Mexico.

La Salle's ship, the <u>Belle</u>, landing at Matagorda Bay on the western shores of the Gulf of Mexico in 1685. It would be La Salle's last expedition.

On February 18, 1685, the *Belle* landed. Then the *Amiable* started through a narrow channel that led into Matagorda Bay, but instead of following the channel, she landed on shoals and sank.

Lost with the ship were most of the expedition's food supplies, sixty barrels of wine, four cannons, most of the tools, a forge, a mill, boxes of arms, nearly all the medicines, and most of the baggage of the soldiers and colonists.

La Salle's company of dejected men and homesick women camped on the swampy shore of Matagorda Bay. Without ovens, they boiled the flour they had saved from the wreck in water to make a sort of porridge for meals. Almost everyone became sick with dysentery after eating the spoiled food and drinking the brackish water. Five or six sick men died every day.

It soon became clear even to La Salle that they were nowhere near the Mississippi River. It would have been sensible to withdraw, sail back to Santo Domingo, and start all over again. But La Salle was stubborn. He had overcome terrible conditions on his previous expeditions, and he was determined to do so again.

So he had no objections when Captain Beaujeu, having completed his mission of landing La Salle on the Gulf of Mexico, decided to return home. On March 12, the *Joly* sailed for France, leaving La Salle and his colonists at Matagorda Bay. One ship, the *Belle*, remained with him.

After scouting the area, La Salle decided to build a fort about five miles (three kilometers) inland on the banks of a creek, away from the unhealthy swamps of the bay. It was difficult to construct because there were no trees nearby. Without horses or oxen, the men had to drag tree trunks by hand over long distances before they could cut them up for lumber. The carpenters he brought from France proved incompetent, so La Salle himself directed the construction. When it was completed, he named it Fort St. Louis, the same name he had given to an earlier fort on the Illinois River.

The Fifth Expedition

With his base secure, La Salle, accompanied by fifty men, set out in October on an exploratory journey. They marched into the interior of what is now Texas, meeting mostly hostile Indians along the way. Their scouting mission found no sign of the Mississippi River. Five months later, in March 1686, La Salle returned to Fort St. Louis, with only a handful of the men he had started out with. Many had died during the journey.

There he learned more distressing news. His only remaining ship, the *Belle*, had been wrecked on a sandbar. Her captain had been drunk and the crew careless. With the loss of the *Belle* went his only hope of sending back for more supplies or escaping from the unhealthy climate of the settlement.

Of the 180 colonists who had landed the year before, only forty-five remained. Most of the others had died; some had deserted. Morale was low, and many settlers grumbled about La Salle's leadership. Parkman described the scene:

> *The weary precincts of Fort St. Louis, with its fences of rigid palisades, its area of trampled earth, its buildings of weather-stained timber, and its well-peopled graveyard without, were hateful to their sight. La Salle had a heavy task to save them from despair. His composure, his unfailing equanimity, his words of encouragement and cheer, were the breath of life to this forlorn community.*

La Salle knew that a journey back to French settlements for more supplies was the only way to save the new colony. He decided to lead a party by land to the Illinois River and eventually Canada—a journey of three thousand miles (1,800 kilometers).

NINE

The Death of La Salle

On January 12, 1687, La Salle marched out of Fort St. Louis on his last trip, leading a group of twenty men, with five horses carrying supplies. Left behind were twenty men, women, and children to wait for his return.

In La Salle's party were his brother, Abbé Jean Cavelier; two young nephews named Moranget and Cavelier; a trusted lieutenant, Henri Joutel; his faithful companion Nika, the Shawnee; and about a dozen woodsmen, soldiers, and trappers.

Ahead was a long journey north and east before they reached the familiar Mississippi River. The country was not easy to cross. Day after day, they marched though tall grass, waded through stagnant water, and used their axes to cut passages for the horses. They hunted buffalo for food and used the hides to make shoes.

It was an unhappy group, not only because of the difficulties of the march but because of stored-up grievances. The men were angry at La Salle's stern commands and what they saw as rude behavior on the part of his young nephews.

That resentment came to a head in mid-March, when the expedition reached the vicinity of the Trinity River, about a third of the way to the Mississippi River. It was a minor matter, but it led to tragedy. As provisions grew low, La Salle sent seven men, including Nika, ahead to a place where on a previous expedition he had stored some corn and beans. When the men got there, they found that the food had rotted. On the way back, though, Nika shot two buffalo, thus assuring the party of plenty to eat. They sent a message to La Salle, asking him to dispatch help to carry the buffalo meat back. He sent the horses under the command of his nephew Moranget. It was a fatal mistake.

When Moranget arrived, he found one of the men, Duhaut, smoking the meat to preserve it. As was the custom of the time, Duhaut, the smoker, had reserved some of it for himself. Moranget, a hot-tempered young man, rebuked Duhaut and seized the meat.

In a rage, Duhaut and one of his companions, Liotot, decided on revenge. That night, as Moranget was sleeping, Liotot took an axe, and with rapid blows used it to kill Moranget, Nika, and a third man. The murderers knew that they would be in serious trouble when La Salle discovered the crime. They resolved to murder him, too.

Their opportunity came the next day, March 19, when La Salle and Joutel came to look for the food party. As La Salle approached, Duhaut and Liotot hid in the tall grass. Another one of their gang walked forward to meet him.

"Where is my nephew?" La Salle asked.

"Gone to the dogs," replied the man.

As La Salle continued to advance, two shots rang out from Duhaut and Liotot, hidden in the grass. La Salle dropped, hit in the head. He died instantly. The two murderers dragged him into the brush, stripped

The assassination of La Salle on May 19, 1687, painted much later by George Catlin.

off his clothes, and left his body "a prey to buzzards and wolves."

> *Thus in the vigor of his manhood, at the age of forty-three, died Robert Cavelier de la Salle. . . . without question one of the most remarkable explorers whose names live in history.*

So wrote Francis Parkman, his most eminent biographer.

We know all the details of the murder of La Salle because Joutel described them when he returned to France.

What happened to the murderers of La Salle?

Joutel reported their fate. Shortly after La Salle's death, they quarreled with two other men in the expedition, who shot and killed them.

What happened to the colonists left behind in Fort St. Louis?

In January 1688, an Indian war party made a surprise attack, killing almost everyone. Six children were saved by Indian women, who raised them as their own. Years later they were turned over to the

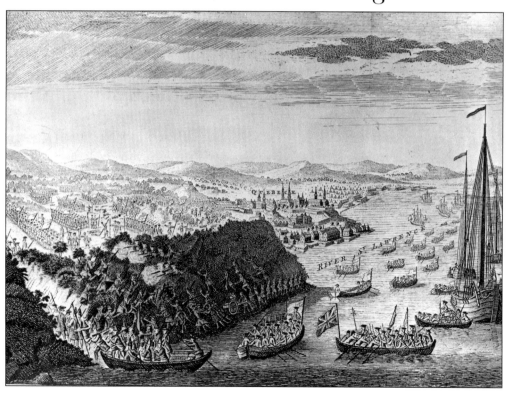

A view of Quebec in 1759, when it was captured by the English—a key event in the loss of French Canada to England.

Spanish. Two of the older boys were enrolled in the Spanish Navy. In 1696, they were captured by the French and returned to their homeland. The others presumably remained in Spain.

What happened to La Salle's vision of a thriving Louisiana?

Not long after his death, two brothers, Pierre le Moyne d'Iberville and Jean-Baptiste le Moyne de Bienville, established permanent French colonies at Mobile Bay, Biloxi, and New Orleans. But when Quebec fell to the British in 1759, the French lost interest in America. In 1762, they ceded Louisiana to Spain.

Things changed in 1803. For a brief time, France regained possession of Louisiana, but in that same year, they sold it to the Americans in an agreement known as the Louisiana Purchase, and it became part of the United States.

Today we can say that La Salle's vision has become a reality—the Mississippi River is one of the main arteries of commerce in the United States, and the entire area of its watershed is the heart of a prosperous nation.

La Salle and His Times

1643 Born in Rouen, France.

1666 Leaves for Canada, establishes trading center at La Chine, west of Montreal.

1669 First expedition: to the Ohio River.

1673 Builds Fort Frontenac on Lake Ontario.

1674 Returns to France, raised to rank of nobleman, returns to Canada.

1676 Rebuilds Fort Frontenac.

1677 Once more returns to France, raises money for new settlements.

1679 Second expedition: builds the *Griffin* on Lake Erie; reaches Illinois River, builds Fort Crèvecoeur on the Illinois River.

1680 Third expedition: gets first sight of Mississippi River.

1681–1682 Fourth expedition: travels down entire length of Mississippi River to the Gulf of Mexico.

1683 Returns to France; King Louis approves building fort at mouth of the Mississippi.

1684 Fifth expedition: by sea to the Gulf of Mexico.

1685 Lands on Texas shore.

1687 Tries to go overland to the Mississippi; is murdered.

FURTHER RESEARCH

Books

For those who want to read more about the early exploration of America and the beginnings of United States history, the following books may be helpful.

Faber, Harold. *From Sea to Sea: The Growth of the United States.* New York: Scribner's, 1992.

———. *The Discoverers of America.* New York: Scribner's, 1992.

Faber, Harold, and Doris Faber. *We the People: The Story of the United States Constitution Since 1787.* New York: Scribner's, 1987.

———. *The Birth of a Nation: The Early Years of the United States.* New York: Scribner's, 1989.

Jacobs, W. J. *Robert Cavelier de La Salle.* New York: Franklin Watts, 1975.

Lomask, Milton. *Great Lives: Exploration.* New York, Scribner's: 1988.

For Older Readers

Morison, Samuel Eliot. *The European Discovery of America. The Northern Voyages.* New York: Oxford, 1971.

Muhlstein, Anka. *La Salle: Explorer of the North American Frontier.* New York: Arcade, 1994

Parkman, Francis. *La Salle and the Discovery of the Great West.* New York: Signet, 1924.

Websites

The Explorers: Cavalier de La Salle
   http://www.vmnf.civilization.ca/Explor/lasal_e1.html

Further Research

The La Salle Shipwreck Project
   Texas Historical Commission
   http://www.thc.state.tx.us/belle/

BIBLIOGRAPHY

Bakeless, John. *America as Seen by Its First Explorers.* New York: Dover, 1989.

Baxter, James Phinney. *A Memoir of Jacques Cartier.* New York: Dodd, Mead, 1906.

Bishop, Morris. *Champlain: The Life of Fortitude.* New York: Knopf, 1948.

Braider, Donald. *The Niagara.* New York: Holt, Rinehart and Winston, 1972.

Caruso, John Anthony. *The Mississippi Valley Frontier.* New York: Bobbs Merrill, 1966.

Ferris, Robert G., editor. *Explorers and Settlers.* Washington, D.C.: National Park Service, 1968.

Finley, John. *The French in the Heart of America.* New York: Scribner's, 1918.

Jacobs, W.J. *Robert Cavelier de La Salle.* New York: Franklin Watts, 1975.

Jennings, David. *The Invasion of America.* New York: Norton, 1975.

Keats, John. *Eminent Domain: The Louisiana Purchase and the Making of America.* New York: Charterhouse, 1973.

Lomask, Milton: *Exploration.* New York: Scribner's, 1988.

Morison, Samuel Eliot. *The European Discovery of America: The Northern Voyages.* Volume 1. New York: Oxford, 1971.

Muhlstein, Anka. *La Salle: Explorer of the North American Frontier.* New York: Arcade, 1994.

Parkman, Francis. *The Discovery of the Great West: La Salle.* New York: Rinehart, 1956.

———. *Pioneers of France in the New World.* Boston: Little, Brown, 1924

Quinn, David B. *North America: From Earliest Discovery to First Settlement.* New York: Harper and Row, 1977.

Solomon, Louis. *The Mississippi: America's Mainstream.* New York: McGraw Hill, 1971.

Thwaites, Ruben Gold. *France in America.* New York: Haskell, 1969.

SOURCE NOTES

13 *"He is a restless boy"*: Anka Muhlstein, *LaSalle: Explorer of the North American Frontier* (Arcade, 1994), p. 4.

20 *"One doesn't wear. . . ."*: Muhlstein, p. 25.

27 *"If the weather is fair. . . ."*: Francis Parkman, *The Great Discovery of the West* (Rinehart, 1956), pp. 13-14.

33 *"It will not be found. . . . "*: Parkman, p.248.

33 *"If I am wanting. . . ."*: Parkman, p. 251.

35 *"a man of intelligence. . . ."*: Parkman, p. 74.

36 *"If he had preferred. . . ."*: Parkman, p. 84.

37 *"great intelligence and good sense"*: Muhlstein, p. 84.

37 *"Louis, by the grace. . . ."*: Parkman, p. 91.

39 *"His brothers and relations. . . ."*: Parkman, p. 93.

40 *"We entered the beautiful river. . . ."*: Donald Braider, *The Niagara* (Holt, Rinehart and Winston, 1972), pp. 48-49.

47 *"In those early French. . . ."*: Parkman, p. 132.

50 *"During sixty-five days. . . ."*: Parkman, p.146. (Parkman does not identify the chronicler to whom he refers.)

52 *"They are politically minded. . . ."*: Muhlstein, p. 127.

53 *"I have never suffered. . . ."*: John Anothony Caruso, *The Mississippi Valley Frontier* (Bobbs, Merrill, 1962), p. 172.

55 *"I was never. . . ."*: Parkman, p.169.

55 *"The Sieur de La Salle. . . ."*: Parkman, p. 233.

56 *"In the name of. . . ."*: Parkman, pp. 225-26.

58 *"Though my discovery is made. . . ."*: Parkman, p. 229.

68 *"The weary precincts. . . ."*: Parkman, p. 307.

70–1 *"Where is my nephew?" "Gone to the dogs." "a prey to buzzards and wolves"*: Muhlstein, p. 210.

71 *"Thus in the vigor. . . ."*: Parkman, p. 317.

INDEX

Page numbers in boldface are illustrations.